FOCUS ON

MIDDLE SCHOOL

Physics

Laboratory Workbook

Rebecca W. Keller, PhD

Cover design: David Keller
Opening page: David Keller, Rebecca W. Keller, PhD
Illustrations: Rebecca W. Keller, PhD

Focus On Middle School Physics Laboratory Workbook
ISBN 978-1-936114-66-5

Published by Gravitas Publications, Inc.
www.gravitaspublications.com

Keeping a Laboratory Notebook

A laboratory notebook is essential for the experimental scientist. In this type of notebook, the results of all the experiments are kept together along with comments and any additional information that is gathered. For this curriculum, you should use this workbook as your laboratory notebook and record your experimental observations and conclusions directly on its pages, just as a real scientist would.

The experimental section for each chapter is pre-written. The exact format of a notebook may vary among scientists, but all experiments written in a laboratory notebook have certain essential parts. For each experiment, a descriptive but short *Title* is written at the top of the page along with the *Date* the experiment is performed. Below the title, an *Objective* and a *Hypothesis* are written. The objective is a short statement that tells something about why you are doing the experiment, and the hypothesis is the predicted outcome. Next, a *Materials List* is written. The materials needed for the experiment should be gathered before the experiment is started.

Following the *Materials List* is the *Experiment*. The sequence of steps and all the details for performing the experiment are written beforehand. Any changes made during the experiment should be written down. Include all information that might be of some importance. For example, if you are to measure 237 ml (1 cup) of water for an experiment, but you actually measured 296 ml (1 1/4 cup), this should be recorded. It is hard sometimes to predict the way in which even small variations in an experiment will affect the outcome, and it is easier to track a problem if all of the information is recorded.

The next section is the *Results* section. Here you will record your experimental observations. It is extremely important that you be honest about what is observed. For example, if the experimental instructions say that a solution will turn yellow, but your solution turned blue, you must record blue. You may have done the experiment incorrectly, or you might have discovered a new and interesting result, but either way, it is very important that your observations be honestly recorded.

Finally, the *Conclusions* should be written. Here you will explain what the observations may mean. You should try to write only *valid* conclusions. It is important to learn to think about what the data actually show and also what cannot be concluded from the experiment.

Laboratory Safety

Most of these experiments use household items. Extra care should be taken while working with all materials in this series of experiments. The following are some general laboratory precautions that should be applied to the home laboratory:

▸ Never put things in your mouth without explicit instructions to do so. This means that food items should not be eaten unless tasting or eating is part of the experiment.

▸ Wear safety glasses while using glass objects or strong chemicals such as bleach.

▸ Wash hands before and after handling all chemicals.

▸ Use adult supervision while working with electricity and glassware, and while performing any step requiring a stove.

Contents

Experiment 1: It's the Law!   Date: _____

Objective   In this experiment we will use the scientific method to determine Newton's First Law of Motion.

Hypothesis   _____

              _____

Materials

    tennis ball
    yarn or string (3 meters [10 ft])
    paper clip
    marble

Experiment

PART I

❶ Take the tennis ball outside, and throw it as far as you can. Observe how the ball travels through the air. In the space below, sketch the path of the ball.

❷ Now, take the string or yarn and, using the paper clip, attach it to the tennis ball. To do this, open the paper clip up on one side and curve the end as follows:

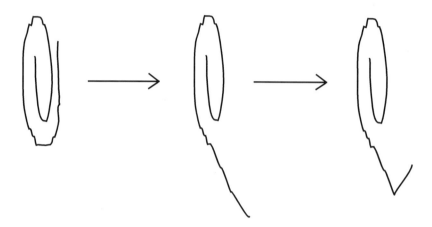

❸ Put the extended curved end of the paper clip into the tennis ball by gently pushing and twisting.

❹ Next, tie the string to the end of the paper clip.

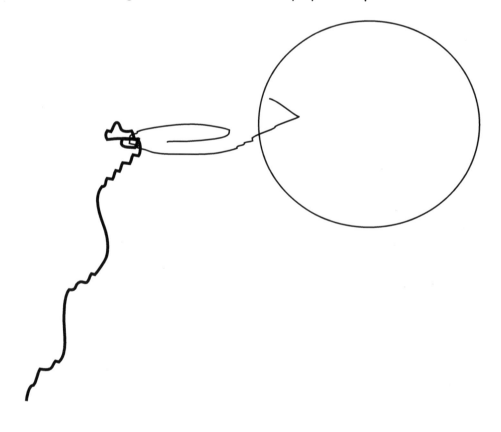

❺ Holding onto one end of the string, again throw the ball into the air as far as you can. Note how the ball travels and, in the space below, record what you see. Do this several times.

Part II

❶ Take the marble and find a straight, clear path on a smooth area of the floor or outdoors. Roll the marble, and record how it travels. Note where and how it stops or changes direction. Do this several times, and record your observations in the next box.

❷   Repeat Step 1 using a rough surface on which to roll the marble.

Conclusions

Draw some conclusions about your results and record them below.

_____

_____

_____

_____

_____

_____

_____

_____

_____

_____

_____

_____

_____

_____

Review

Define the following:

physics _____

_____

physical law _____

_____

List the 5 steps of the scientific method

1 _____

2 _____

3 _____

4 _____

5 _____

Experiment 2: Fruit Works?   Date: _____

Read through all the steps of this experiment. Then write an objective and a hypothesis.

Objective   _____

                 _____

Hypothesis   _____

                 _____

Materials

    Slinky
    several paper clips
    1-2 apples
    1-2 lemons or limes
    1-2 oranges
    1-2 bananas
    spring balance scale or food scale
    meter stick (or yardstick) or tape measure
    tape

Experiment

❶ Try to determine, just by "weighing" each piece of fruit in your hands, which piece will do the most work and which piece will do the least work on the spring that is in the scale.

❷ State your prediction as the hypothesis.

❸ Next, weigh each piece of fruit on the balance or food scale.

❹ Record the weights in the following chart.

Fruit	Weight (grams or ounces)

❺ Prepare the fruit for the experiment. Take a paper clip and stretch one side out to make a small hook like you did in Experiment 1. Place the hook in one of the pieces of fruit.

Repeat for each different kind of fruit you will be testing.

❻ Next, take the Slinky and hold it up to the level of your chest. Allow 10 to 15 coils to hang below your hand. You will have to hold most of the Slinky in your hand.

❼ Measure the distance from the floor to the bottom of the Slinky with the meter stick, yardstick, or tape measure. Record your result below.

Distance from floor to Slinky with no fruit attached

❽ Take a piece of fruit with a hook in it and attach it to the end of the Slinky. Hold the Slinky at the same height as in Step 6 with the same number of coils hanging below your hand. Allow the Slinky to be pulled down by the fruit.

❾ Use the meter stick, yardstick, or tape measure to measure from the end of the Slinky to the floor. Record your results in the following chart in the *Distance Floor to Slinky (With Fruit)* column.

❿ Repeat Steps 8 and 9 with different kinds of fruit. Record your results each time.

Results

❶ In each row of the *Distance Floor to Slinky (No Fruit)* column, write the distance you recorded in Step 7. Then subtract this distance from each of the distances you recorded in the *Distance Floor to Slinky (With Fruit)* column. This gives you the distance the Slinky was extended by each piece of fruit.

Fruit	Distance Floor to Slinky (With Fruit)	Distance Floor to Slinky (No Fruit)	Distance Extended

❷ Calculate the work each piece of fruit has done. Record your answers in the following chart.

Fruit	Work

❸ What would happen if you attached two pieces of the same kind of fruit to the Slinky? How much work would be done?

Prediction _____

_____

_____

_____

❹ Test your prediction and calculate the work that was done by the two pieces of fruit. Record your data in the charts below.

2 Pieces of Fruit	Weight	Distance: Floor to Slinky (With Fruit)	Distance Floor to Slinky (No Fruit)	Distance Extended

2 Pieces of Fruit	Work

Conclusions

Draw some conclusions about your results and record them below.

_____

_____

_____

_____

_____

_____

_____

_____

_____

_____

_____

_____

_____

_____

_____

Review

Define the following terms:

force _____

_____

work _____

_____

energy _____

_____

In the following pairs of items, which object has the greater gravitational force? (Circle the correct answer in each pair.)

a banana or a bowling ball
a car or a bicycle
the Moon or the Earth
the Earth or the Sun

Answer the following questions:

▸ Is a book sitting on a shelf doing work? _____

▸ Is a bowling ball crashing into the pins doing work? _____

▸ How much work is done if you lift a 3 kg box 2 meters (or a 6.6 lb box 6.6 feet)? _____

▸ How much work is done if you lift a 2 kg box 3 meters (or 4.4 lb box 9.9 feet)? _____

List some forms of energy:

_____   _____   _____

Challenge:

Do you think that if we could get every person on the Earth to jump all at once, we could move the Earth? Why or why not? Can you do a rough calculation to test your theory?

Experiment 3: Smashed Banana   Date: _____

Objective   _____

               _____

Hypothesis   _____

               _____

Materials

　　　small to medium size toy car
　　　stiff cardboard
　　　wooden board (more than 1 meter [3 feet] long)
　　　straight pin or tack
　　　small scale or balance
　　　1 banana, sliced
　　　10 pennies
　　　meter stick, yardstick, or tape measure
　　　tape

Experiment

❶   Read through all the steps of this experiment. Then write an objective and a hypothesis.

❷   Take a portion of the cardboard to make a backing for the banana slices. Using a straight pin or tack, attach a banana slice to the cardboard near the bottom.

❸   Use the wooden board to make a ramp. One end of the ramp should meet the banana slice. Your setup should look like the following illustration.

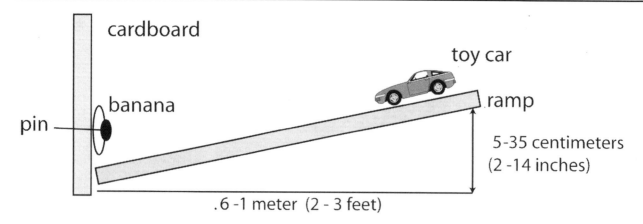

❹   Weigh the toy car with the scale or balance. Record your result.

Weight of toy car (grams or ounces) = _____

❺   Place the toy car on the ramp and elevate one end of the ramp 5 centimeters (2 inches). Allow the toy car to roll down the ramp and hit the banana. Record your results in the following chart.

❻   Elevate the ramp another 5 cm (two inches). Now the ramp should be 10 cm (4 inches) off the ground. Allow the toy car to roll down the ramp and hit the banana. Record your results in the chart below

❼   Repeat, elevating the ramp 5 centimeters (2 inches) more each time. Record your results in the following chart.

Height (centimeters or inches)	Results (write your comments)
5 centimeters (2 inches)	
10 centimeters (4 inches)	
15 centimeters (6 inches)	
20 centimeters (8 inches)	
25 centimeters (10 inches)	
30 centimeters (12 inches)	
35 centimeters (14 inches)	

❽   Answer the following questions:

What happened to the speed of the car as the ramp height increased?

_____

At which ramp height did the car smash the banana?

_____

❾   Now add 10 pennies to the toy car and weigh it again. Repeat the previous steps, rolling the toy car with the pennies on it down the ramp and elevating the ramp 5 centimeters (2 inches) more each time Record your results.

Weight of toy car plus 10 pennies (grams or ounces) = _____

Height (centimeters or inches)	Results (write your comments)
5 centimeters (2 inches)	
10 centimeters (4 inches)	
15 centimeters (6 inches)	
20 centimeters (8 inches)	
25 centimeters (10 inches)	
30 centimeters (12 inches)	
35 centimeters (14 inches)	

❿   Answer the following questions:

At which ramp height did the car smash the banana? _____

Was the banana smashed at the same height by the light car and the heavy car? _____

If "no," which car needed to be at a greater height to smash the banana? _____

Results

Calculate the GPE for the height of the ramp at which the toy car—with and without the 10 pennies—smashed the banana. Use the equation:

gravitational potential energy (GPE) = weight x height

Record your answers below.

GPE for car without pennies _____

GPE for car with pennies _____

Is the GPE the same (or close to the same) for both cars? _____

Conclusions

_____

_____

_____

_____

_____

_____

_____

_____

_____

_____

_____

_____

_____

_____

_____

_____

_____

Review

Define the following terms:

potential energy _____

_____

gravitational potential energy _____

_____

chemical potential energy _____

_____

kinetic energy _____

_____

Fill in the blanks for the following measurements:

1 foot = _____ inches

1 yard = _____ feet

1 mile = _____ yards

1 meter = _____ centimeters

1 centimeter = _____ millimeters

1 gram = _____ kilogram

1 pound = _____ ounces

Experiment 4: Moving Marbles

Date: _____

Objective _____

_____

Hypothesis _____

_____

Materials

several glass marbles of different sizes
steel marbles of different sizes
cardboard tube, .7–1 meter (2 1/2–3 ft) long
scissors
black marking pen
ruler
letter scale or other small scale or balance

Experiment

❶ Using the scale, weigh each of the marbles, both glass and steel. Label the marbles with numbers or letters, or note their colors, so that you can keep track of how much each marble weighs. Record your results in **Part A** of the *Results* section.

❷ Take the cardboard tube and cut it in half lengthwise to make a trough. Measure the length of the tube, and mark the halfway point with the black marking pen.

❸ Beginning at the halfway mark, measure .3 meter (1 foot) in both directions, and put a mark at each of these measurements. This will give you one mark on each side of the halfway mark.

❹ The cardboard tube should now have three marks: one at the halfway point, and one on either side of the halfway mark, .3 meter (1 foot) away from it. The tube will be used as a track for the marbles.

❺ Take the marbles and, one by one, roll them down the tube. Notice how each one rolls (Does it roll straight? Is it easy to push off with your thumb? Does it pass the marks you drew?) In **Part B** of the *Results* section, describe how each marble rolls.

❻ Now place a glass marble on the center mark of the tube.

❼ Roll a glass marble of the same size toward the marble in the center. Watch the two marbles as they collide. Record your results in the *Results* section, **Part C**.

❽ Repeat Steps 6 and 7 with different size marbles. For example, try rolling a heavy marble toward a light marble and a light marble toward a heavy marble. Record your results in **Part D**.

Results

Part A

Marble	Weight

Part B

_____

_____

_____

_____

_____

_____

_____

_____

_____

_____

Part C

_____

_____

_____

_____

_____

_____

_____

_____

Part D

_____

_____

_____

_____

_____

_____

_____

Conclusions

Review

Define the following terms:

inertia _____

_____

mass _____

_____

momentum_____

_____

friction _____

_____

▸ Write the equation for momentum:

_____

▸ Which has more mass: a bowling ball or a green pea? (circle one)

▸ Which has more momentum: a rolling bowling ball or

a bowling ball shot from a cannon? (circle one)

Experiment 5: Power Pennies

Date: _____

Objective _____

_____

Hypothesis _____

_____

Materials

10-20 copper pennies
aluminum foil
paper towels
salt water: 30-45 ml (2-3 Tbsp.) salt per 240 ml (1 cup) water
voltmeter
2 plastic-coated copper wires, each 10-15 cm (4"-6") long
duct tape (or other strong tape)
scissors
wire cutters
steel wool

Experiment

❶   Cut out several penny-sized circles from the aluminum foil and a paper towel.

❷   Soak the paper towel circles in the salt water.

❸   Strip the plastic coating off both ends of one of the pieces of wire, using wire cutters to carefully cut through the plastic without cutting the metal wire. Take one end of the wire and tape the exposed metal to a penny.

❹   Strip the plastic off the ends of the other piece of wire. Tape the exposed metal on one end of the wire to a piece of aluminum foil.

❺ Begin stacking the pieces by placing the circle of aluminum foil with the wire attached wire side down on a firm surface. Put one of the wet paper towel circles on top of the aluminum foil. On top of the paper, place the penny that has the wire taped to it. It should look like this:

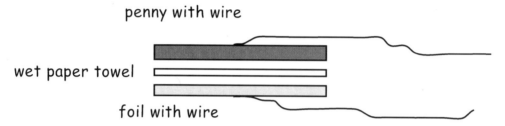

❻ Take the wires and connect them to the leads (wires) of the voltmeter. Switch the voltmeter to "voltage" and record the number it shows. This is the amount of voltage the single layer battery produces.

❼ Add another "cell" to the battery and record the voltage. (A cell is a penny layer, a paper layer, and a foil layer.) The battery now has two cells. It should look like the following:

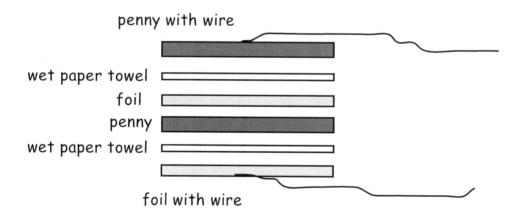

❽ Continue adding cells made of foil, wet paper towel, and pennies, and record the voltage when each new cell is added.

Results

Number of Cells	Voltage
1	
2	
3	
4	
5	

Plot your data. Make a graph with "Voltage" on the x-axis and "Number of Cells" on the y-axis.

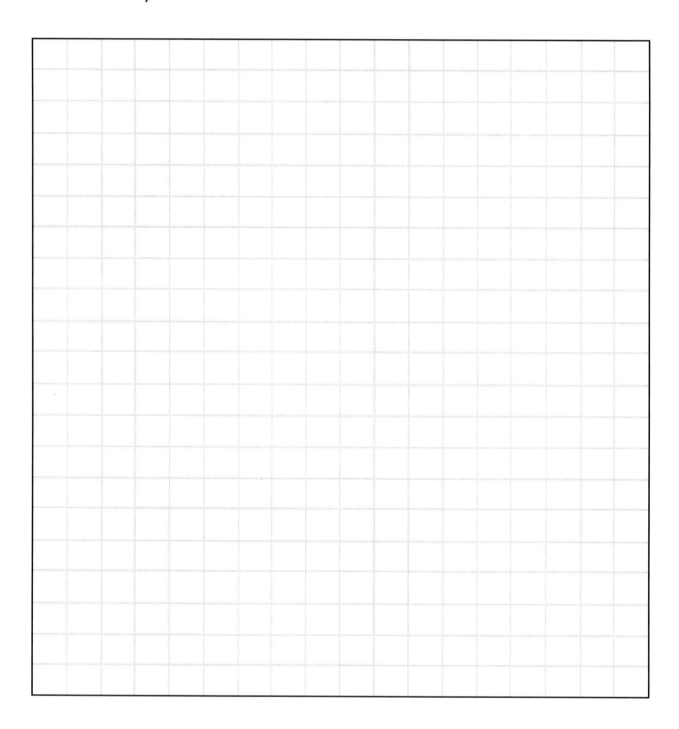

Discuss your data.

_____

_____

_____

_____

_____

_____

_____

_____

_____

_____

_____

_____

_____

_____

_____

_____

Conclusions

_____

_____

_____

_____

_____

_____

_____

_____

_____

_____

_____

_____

_____

_____

_____

_____

Review

Answer the following questions:

▶ What is chemical energy? _____

_____

▶ Name two foods that have "food energy" (carbohydrates).

_____

_____

▶ What are two examples of energy we use for fuel?

_____

_____

▶ Who made the first battery?

_____

Draw a diagram of a voltaic battery.

Experiment 6: Charge It!   Date: _____

Objective _____

_____

Hypothesis _____

_____

Materials

small glass jar with lid
aluminum foil
paper clip
duct tape (or other strong tape)
plastic or rubber rod (or balloon)
silk fabric
scissors
ruler

Experiment

Building an *electroscope* (an instrument that detects electric charge)

❶ Cut two thin strips of aluminum foil of equal length (about 2.5 cm [1 inch] long).

❷ Poke a small hole in the center of the lid of the glass jar.

❸ Open one end of the paper clip to make a small hook.

❹ Place the straightened out piece of the paper clip through the small hole in the jar lid, bend, and secure the paper clip to the lid with strong tape, leaving the end of the paper clip exposed.

❺ Hang the two strips of aluminum foil from the hook that is on the underside of the jar lid. Place the lid on the jar with the aluminum foil hanging from the hook inside the jar.

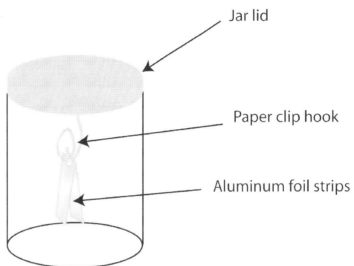

Jar lid

Paper clip hook

Aluminum foil strips

❻ You now have an electroscope.

❼ Take the plastic or rubber rod and rub it with the silk fabric, or take the balloon and rub it in your hair or on the cat.

❽ Gently touch the plastic or rubber rod or the balloon to the end of the paper clip that is sticking out of the jar lid.

❾ Observe the two pieces of aluminum foil and record your results.

Results

_____

_____

_____

_____

_____

_____

_____

_____

_____

_____

_____

_____

_____

_____

_____

_____

_____

Conclusions

_____

_____

_____

_____

_____

_____

_____

_____

_____

_____

_____

_____

_____

_____

_____

_____

_____

Review

Define the following terms:

dry cell _____

_____

electric charge _____

_____

electrical force _____

_____

friction _____

_____

Circle the correct word to complete the statement:

▸   Like charges (repel / attract) each other.

▸   Unlike charges (repel / attract) each other.

List the parts of an atom and whether or not they are charged.

_____

_____

_____

Experiment 7: Let It Flow

Date: _____

Objective   _____

_____

Hypothesis   _____

_____

Materials

1.2 meters (4 ft) insulated electrical wire
6v or larger battery
insulating materials (such as styrofoam, plastic, cloth, etc.)
small light bulb
electrical tape
several small resistors
scissors
wire cutters

Experiment

❶   Cut the wire into two pieces, each about .3 meter (1 foot) long. Carefully shave the ends of the plastic insulation from the ends of the wires to expose the metal. Leave about 6-12 mm (1/4 to 1/2 inch) of exposed metal on each end.

❷   Tape one end of one wire to the positive (+) terminal of the battery. Tape one end of the other wire to the negative (-) terminal of the battery. Alligator clips can be used instead of electrical tape to fasten the wires to the battery terminals.

❸   Tape the other ends of the two wires to the light bulb. One wire should be taped to the bottom of the bulb, and the other one should be taped to the metal side of the bulb.

Record your results on the chart in the *Results* section.

❹ Remove the end of one wire from the battery and gently touch it with your finger to see if it is warm.

Record your results.

❺ Now place a piece of styrofoam or plastic in between one wire and the bulb.

Record your results.

❻ Remove the end of one wire from the battery and gently touch it with your finger to see if it is warm.

Record your results.

❼ Place a resistor between the light bulb and the battery on one wire. Observe any difference in the intensity of the light bulb.

Record your results in the chart.

Repeat with two or more resistors.

❽ Remove one end of the wire from the battery and gently touch it with your finger to see if it is warm.

Record your results.

Results

	wire only	wire + insulator	wire + resistor(s)
light bulb intensity			
temperature of wire			

Answer the following questions about your experiment:

▸ What happened when you connected the battery to the light bulb?

_____

_____

▸ What happened when you put a piece of styrofoam or plastic between the wire and the bulb?

_____

_____

▸ What happened when you put one or more resistors between the light bulb and the battery?

_____

_____

▸ What did the wire feel like to your fingers (with the wire only, with the insulator, and with the resistors)?

_____

_____

_____

Conclusions

_____

_____

_____

_____

_____

_____

_____

_____

_____

_____

_____

_____

_____

_____

_____

Review

Define the following:

static electricity _____

_____

electric current _____

_____

voltage _____

_____

resistor _____

_____

conductor _____

_____

insulator _____

_____

heat _____

_____

Experiment 8: Wrap It Up!   Date: _____

Objective   _____

_____

Hypothesis   _____

_____

Materials

metal rod (a large nail or a screwdriver can be used)
electrical wire
10-20 paper clips
6v or larger battery
electrical tape
scissors
wire cutters

Experiment

❶ Cut the electrical wire so that it is .3-.6 meter (1-2 feet) long.

❷ Trim the plastic coating off the wire so that there is about 6 mm (1/4 inch) of exposed metal on each end of the wire.

❸ Tape one end of the wire to the positive (+) terminal of the battery. (Alligator clips may be used in place of tape.)

❹ Tape the other end of the wire to the negative (-) terminal of the battery.

❺ Take the metal rod and touch it to the paper clips. Record your results on the chart in the *Results* section.

❻ Coil the wire around the metal rod a few times. The wire must remain hooked to the battery.

❼   Touch the metal rod to the paper clips. Count the coils and record your results.

❽   Wrap another 1 to 5 coils around the metal rod.

❾   Touch the end of the metal rod to the paper clips. Record how many paper clips can be picked up.

❿   Continue adding coils to the metal rod and counting the number of paper clips that can be picked up. Record the results each time you increase the number of coils.

Results

Number of Coils	Number of Paper Clips

Graph your results.

Conclusions

_____

_____

_____

_____

_____

_____

_____

_____

_____

_____

_____

_____

_____

_____

_____

_____

_____

Review

What makes materials magnetic? _____

_____

Why are some materials magnetic and others not? _____

_____

What are poles? _____

_____

Opposite poles (attract / repel). [Circle the correct word.]

Like poles (attract / repel). [Circle the correct word.]

What happens if an electric current flows around a metal rod?

_____

_____

What happens if a magnetic rod is pushed and pulled through a wire coil?

_____

_____

Draw a magnetic field.

Experiment 9: Bending Light and Circle Sounds

Date: _____

Objective

_____

_____

Hypothesis

_____

_____

Materials

two prisms (glass or plastic)
flashlight
metal can, open at both ends
aluminum foil
rubber band
laser pointer
long wooden craft stick
colored pencils
duct tape (or other strong tape)

Experiment

PART I: Bending Light

❶ Take one prism and shine the flashlight beam through it at the 90° bend. (See following illustration.) Have a wall or white board behind the prism.

Record your results in the *Results* section.

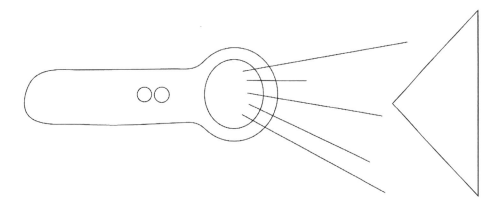

❷ Now take the prism and let sunlight shine through it from the same direction.

Record your results.

❸ Take the second prism and place it directly behind the first one, laying it flat on one of the short edges. Using the flashlight, shine light through the two prisms together. (See illustration.)

Record your results.

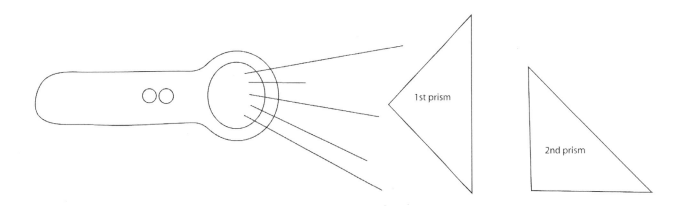

1st prism

2nd prism

Results

PART I: Bending Light

What happens when you shine a flashlight through the prism?

_____

_____

_____

What happens when you put the prism in sunlight?

_____

_____

_____

What happens when you shine light through two prisms at the same time?

_____

_____

_____

Draw the shapes you see.

PART II: Circle Sounds

Assemble and experiment with a "soundscope."

❶ Take the metal can and make sure it is completely open on both ends.

❷ Place a piece of aluminum foil over one end of the can, and secure it with a rubber band. Be careful not to wrinkle the foil; try to keep it smooth.

❸ Fasten the craft stick securely to the metal can with strong tape.

❹ Place the laser pointer on the craft stick with the light facing the foil. It should look like the setup in the following diagram.

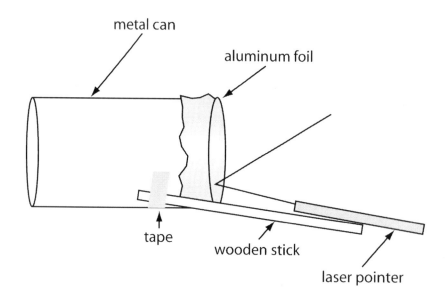

❺ Turn on the laser pointer. (Be careful not to point the laser directly into your eyes!) Observe the reflection on a wall or white board.

❻ Holding the can to your mouth, speak into it, and watch what happens to the reflected laser light. Record your results on the next page.

❼ Continue to speak or sing into the can, recording as many different shapes as you see.

Draw what you see.

Conclusions

PART I: Bending Light

_____

_____

_____

_____

_____

_____

_____

_____

PART II: Circle Sounds

_____

_____

_____

_____

_____

_____

_____

Review

Define the following terms:

electromagnetic wave _____

_____

wavelength _____

_____

amplitude _____

_____

electromagnetic spectrum _____

_____

visible light _____

_____

pitch _____

_____

frequency _____

_____

Are radio waves sound?

_____

Experiment 10: On Your Own   Date: _____

▸ This time you get to design your own experiment. The goal is to convert as many forms of energy as you can into other forms of energy.

Example:

A scenario can be designed in which energy is used to put out a fire. A marble is rolled down a ramp and bumps into a domino that has a small cap of baking soda on top of it. A chemical reaction is started when the baking soda falls into vinegar, which produces carbon dioxide gas that puts out the fire.

In this case, the rolling marble has kinetic energy which is used to convert gravitational potential energy into kinetic energy (the falling baking soda) which then starts a chemical reaction.

Using Energy to Put Out a Fire

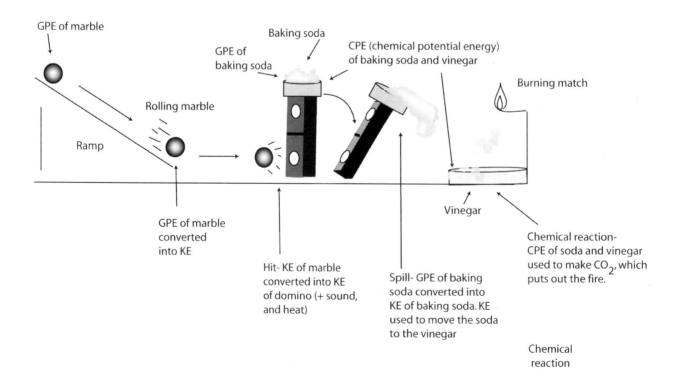

Use the following guide to design your experiment:

❶   Write down all the different forms of energy you can think of.
   kinetic energy

   _____   _____

   _____   _____

   _____   _____

❷   Write down how these forms of energy can be represented.

   kinetic energy
   _____

rolling marble	*moving toy car*	*moving ball*

❸   Write down ways to connect two or more of these forms of energy and explain how one form will be converted into another.

moving toy car bumps into marble and starts it rolling

_____

_____

_____

_____

_____

_____

_____

_____

_____

_____

_____

❹   Design an experiment to convert one form of energy into another. Give your experiment a title, and write an objective and a hypothesis. Write down the materials you will need, and then write down the steps you will take to collect the results. See how many different forms of energy you can convert. Make careful observations and draw conclusions based on what you observe.

Experiment 10: _____ Date: _____

Objective _____

_____

Hypothesis _____

_____

Materials

_____   _____   _____

_____   _____   _____

_____   _____   _____

Experiment

_____

_____

_____

_____

_____

_____

_____

_____

Results

Conclusions

_____

_____

_____

_____

_____

_____

_____

_____

_____

_____

_____

_____

_____

_____

_____

_____

Review

Describe the law of conservation of energy:

_____

_____

_____

_____

_____

What is the energy that is conserved? (Circle one.)

▸   kinetic energy

▸   potential energy

▸   total energy

▸   chemical energy

What is usable energy?

_____

_____

_____

Name one form of energy that is sometimes unusable.

_____